My
Prayer
Journal

KeyNotes

BARBOUR
PUBLISHING

© 2005 by Barbour Publishing, Inc.

ISBN 978-1-59310-647-8

Compiled by Ellen Caughey.

Published by Barbour Publishing, Inc., P.O. Box 719, Uhrichsville, Ohio 44683
www.barbourbooks.com

Our mission is to publish and distribute inspirational products offering exceptional value and biblical encouragement to the masses.

 Member of the
Evangelical Christian
Publishers Association

Printed in China.
5 4 3 2 1

Rejoice evermore.

Pray without ceasing.

1 THESSALONIANS 5:16–17

And it shall come to pass, that before they call,
I will answer: and while they are yet speaking, I will hear.

ISAIAH 65:24

New prayer requests: _____

Date: _____

Ongoing prayer requests: _____

Answers to prayer: ───────────────────────

Praises: ───────────────────────

For every one that asketh receiveth; and he that seeketh findeth;
and to him that knocketh it shall be opened.

MATTHEW 7:8

New prayer requests: _____

_____
_____
_____
_____
_____
_____
_____
_____
_____
_____
_____
_____

Ongoing prayer requests: _____

_____
_____
_____
_____
_____
_____
_____
_____
_____
_____
_____
_____
_____

Date: _____

Answers to prayer: ―――――――――――――――――

_____
_____
_____
_____
_____
_____
_____
_____
_____
_____
_____
_____

Praises: ―――――――――――――――――――――――

_____
_____
_____
_____
_____
_____
_____
_____
_____
_____
_____
_____

And whatsoever ye shall ask in my name, that will I do,
that the Father may be glorified in the Son.

JOHN 14:13

New prayer requests: _____

Date: _____

Ongoing prayer requests: _____

Answers to prayer: _____

_____

_____

_____

_____

_____

_____

_____

_____

_____

_____

_____

Praises: _____

_____

_____

_____

_____

_____

_____

_____

_____

_____

_____

_____

If ye abide in me, and my words abide in you,
ye shall ask what ye will, and it shall be done unto you.

JOHN 15:7

Date:

New prayer requests:

Ongoing prayer requests:

Answers to prayer: _____

_____

_____

_____

_____

_____

_____

_____

_____

_____

_____

Praises: _____

_____

_____

_____

_____

_____

_____

_____

_____

_____

_____

Let us therefore come boldly unto the throne of grace,
that we may obtain mercy, and find grace to help in time of need.

HEBREWS 4:16

New prayer requests: _____

_____
_____
_____
_____
_____
_____
_____
_____
_____
_____
_____
_____

Date: _____

Ongoing prayer requests: _____

_____
_____
_____
_____
_____
_____
_____
_____
_____
_____
_____
_____

Answers to prayer:

Praises:

He shall call upon me, and I will answer him:

I will be with him in trouble; I will deliver him, and honour him.

PSALM 91:15

New prayer requests: _____

Date: _____

Ongoing prayer requests: _____

Answers to prayer: _____

Praises: _____

The LORD is nigh unto all them that call upon him,
to all that call upon him in truth.

PSALM 145:18

New prayer requests: _____

Date: _____

_____
_____
_____
_____
_____
_____
_____
_____
_____
_____
_____
_____

Ongoing prayer requests: _____

_____
_____
_____
_____
_____
_____
_____
_____
_____
_____
_____
_____
_____

Answers to prayer: ———————————————————

————————————————————————————————
————————————————————————————————
————————————————————————————————
————————————————————————————————
————————————————————————————————
————————————————————————————————
————————————————————————————————
————————————————————————————————
————————————————————————————————
————————————————————————————————
————————————————————————————————

Praises: ————————————————————————————

————————————————————————————————
————————————————————————————————
————————————————————————————————
————————————————————————————————
————————————————————————————————
————————————————————————————————
————————————————————————————————
————————————————————————————————
————————————————————————————————
————————————————————————————————
————————————————————————————————

The Lord is far from the wicked:
but he heareth the prayer of the righteous.

PROVERBS 15:29

New prayer requests:

Date:

Ongoing prayer requests:

Answers to prayer: _____

_____

_____

_____

_____

_____

_____

_____

_____

_____

_____

Praises: _____

_____

_____

_____

_____

_____

_____

_____

_____

_____

_____

Call unto me, and I will answer thee,
and shew thee great and mighty things, which thou knowest not.

JEREMIAH 33:3

New prayer requests: _____

Date: _____

Ongoing prayer requests: _____

Answers to prayer: _____

_____

_____

_____

_____

_____

_____

_____

_____

_____

_____

Praises: _____

_____

_____

_____

_____

_____

_____

_____

_____

_____

_____

Devote yourselves to prayer,
being watchful and thankful.

COLOSSIANS 4:2 NIV

New prayer requests: _____

Date: _____

Ongoing prayer requests: _____

Answers to prayer: _____

_____
_____
_____
_____
_____
_____
_____
_____
_____
_____

Praises: _____

_____
_____
_____
_____
_____
_____
_____
_____
_____
_____

Delight thyself also in the LORD;
and he shall give thee the desires of thine heart.

PSALM 37:4

New prayer requests: _____

Date:

Ongoing prayer requests: _____

Answers to prayer: _____

_____
_____
_____
_____
_____
_____
_____
_____
_____
_____

Praises: _____

_____
_____
_____
_____
_____
_____
_____
_____
_____
_____
_____

But when you pray, go into your room,
close the door and pray to your Father, who is unseen.
Then your Father, who sees what is done in secret, will reward you.

MATTHEW 6:6 NIV

New prayer requests: _____
_____
_____
_____
_____
_____
_____
_____
_____
_____
_____

Date: _____

Ongoing prayer requests: _____
_____
_____
_____
_____
_____
_____
_____
_____
_____
_____
_____
_____

Answers to prayer: _____

_____

_____

_____

_____

_____

_____

_____

_____

Praises: _____

_____

_____

_____

_____

_____

_____

_____

_____

_____

Our help is in the name of the LORD,

who made heaven and earth.

PSALM 124:8

New prayer requests: _____

_____
_____
_____
_____
_____
_____
_____
_____
_____
_____
_____

Date: _____

Ongoing prayer requests: _____

_____
_____
_____
_____
_____
_____
_____
_____
_____
_____
_____

Answers to prayer: _____

Praises: _____

*But my God shall supply all your need according
to his riches in glory by Christ Jesus.*

PHILIPPIANS 4:19

New prayer requests: _____

_____
_____
_____
_____
_____
_____
_____
_____
_____
_____
_____
_____
_____

Date: _____

Ongoing prayer requests: _____

_____
_____
_____
_____
_____
_____
_____
_____
_____
_____
_____
_____
_____

Answers to prayer: _____

_____

_____

_____

_____

_____

_____

_____

_____

_____

Praises: _____

_____

_____

_____

_____

_____

_____

_____

_____

_____

But thanks be to God, who always leads us in triumphal procession in Christ

and through us spreads everywhere the fragrance of the knowledge of him.

2 CORINTHIANS 2:14 NIV

New prayer requests: _____

Date: _____

Ongoing prayer requests: _____

Answers to prayer: ....

_____
_____
_____
_____
_____
_____
_____
_____
_____
_____
_____
_____

Praises: ....

_____
_____
_____
_____
_____
_____
_____
_____
_____
_____
_____
_____
_____

The LORD is nigh unto them that are of a broken heart;
and saveth such as be of a contrite spirit.

PSALM 34:18

Date: _____

New prayer requests: _____

_____
_____
_____
_____
_____
_____
_____
_____
_____
_____
_____
_____

Ongoing prayer requests: _____

_____
_____
_____
_____
_____
_____
_____
_____
_____
_____
_____
_____

Answers to prayer: _____

_____

_____

_____

_____

_____

_____

_____

_____

_____

_____

_____

Praises: _____

_____

_____

_____

_____

_____

_____

_____

_____

_____

_____

_____

_____

Be still, and know that I am God:
I will be exalted among the heathen, I will be exalted in the earth.

PSALM 46:10

New prayer requests: _____

_____
_____
_____
_____
_____
_____
_____
_____
_____
_____
_____
_____
_____
_____

Date: _____

Ongoing prayer requests: _____

_____
_____
_____
_____
_____
_____
_____
_____
_____
_____
_____
_____
_____

Answers to prayer: ⎯⎯⎯⎯⎯⎯⎯⎯⎯⎯⎯⎯⎯⎯⎯⎯⎯⎯⎯⎯⎯⎯

Praises: ⎯⎯⎯⎯⎯⎯⎯⎯⎯⎯⎯⎯⎯⎯⎯⎯⎯⎯⎯⎯⎯⎯⎯⎯⎯⎯⎯⎯⎯

Behold, the LORD's hand is not shortened, that it cannot save;
neither his ear heavy, that it cannot hear.

ISAIAH 59:1

New prayer requests: _____

Date: _____

Ongoing prayer requests: _____

Answers to prayer: _____

_____

_____

_____

_____

_____

_____

_____

_____

_____

_____

Praises: _____

_____

_____

_____

_____

_____

_____

_____

_____

_____

_____

_____

Be careful for nothing; but in every thing by prayer and supplication with thanksgiving let your requests be made known unto God.

PHILIPPIANS 4:6

New prayer requests: _____

Date: _____

Ongoing prayer requests: _____

Answers to prayer: _____

_____

_____

_____

_____

_____

_____

_____

_____

_____

_____

_____

Praises: _____

_____

_____

_____

_____

_____

_____

_____

_____

_____

_____

_____

_____

As for me, I will call upon God; and the LORD shall save me.
Evening, and morning, and at noon, will I pray,
and cry aloud: and he shall hear my voice.

PSALM 55:16–17

New prayer requests: _____

Date: _____

Ongoing prayer requests: _____

Answers to prayer:

Praises:

But without faith it is impossible to please him:
for he that cometh to God must believe that he is,
and that he is a rewarder of them that diligently seek him.

HEBREWS 11:6

New prayer requests: _____

_____
_____
_____
_____
_____
_____
_____
_____
_____
_____

Date: _____

Ongoing prayer requests: _____

_____
_____
_____
_____
_____
_____
_____
_____
_____
_____
_____
_____

Answers to prayer: ....

Praises: ....

The effectual fervent prayer of a righteous man availeth much.

JAMES 5:16

New prayer requests: _____

_____
_____
_____
_____
_____
_____
_____
_____
_____
_____
_____
_____
_____

Date: _____

Ongoing prayer requests: _____

_____
_____
_____
_____
_____
_____
_____
_____
_____
_____
_____
_____

Answers to prayer: _____

_____

_____

_____

_____

_____

_____

_____

_____

_____

_____

_____

Praises: _____

_____

_____

_____

_____

_____

_____

_____

_____

_____

_____

_____

_____

If any of you lack wisdom, let him ask of God, that giveth to all men liberally,

and upbraideth not; and it shall be given him.

JAMES 1:5

New prayer requests:

Date:

Ongoing prayer requests:

Answers to prayer: ⎯⎯⎯⎯⎯⎯⎯⎯⎯⎯⎯⎯⎯⎯

Praises: ⎯⎯⎯⎯⎯⎯⎯⎯⎯⎯⎯⎯⎯⎯⎯⎯⎯⎯

For this cause I bow my knees unto the Father of our Lord Jesus Christ.

EPHESIANS 3:14

Date: _____

New prayer requests: _____

_____

_____

_____

_____

_____

_____

_____

_____

_____

_____

_____

Ongoing prayer requests: _____

_____

_____

_____

_____

_____

_____

_____

_____

_____

_____

_____

_____

Answers to prayer: _____

_____
_____
_____
_____
_____
_____
_____
_____
_____

Praises: _____

_____
_____
_____
_____
_____
_____
_____
_____
_____
_____
_____

LORD, in trouble have they visited thee,

they poured out a prayer when thy chastening was upon them.

ISAIAH 26:16

New prayer requests: _____

Date: _____

Ongoing prayer requests: _____

Answers to prayer: _____

Praises: _____

*Again, I tell you that if two of you on earth agree about anything you ask for,
it will be done for you by my Father in heaven.*

MATTHEW 18:19 NIV

New prayer requests:

Date:

Ongoing prayer requests:

Answers to prayer: _____

Praises: _____

When my soul fainted within me I remembered the Lord:

and my prayer came in unto thee, into thine holy temple.

JONAH 2:7

New prayer requests: _____

Date: _____

Ongoing prayer requests: _____

Answers to prayer: ⸻

⸻

⸻

⸻

⸻

⸻

⸻

⸻

⸻

⸻

⸻

⸻

⸻

Praises: ⸻

⸻

⸻

⸻

⸻

⸻

⸻

⸻

⸻

⸻

⸻

⸻

⸻

Watch ye and pray, lest ye enter into temptation.
The spirit truly is ready, but the flesh is weak.

MARK 14:38

Date:

New prayer requests:

Ongoing prayer requests:

Answers to prayer: _____

_____

_____

_____

_____

_____

_____

_____

_____

_____

Praises: _____

_____

_____

_____

_____

_____

_____

_____

_____

_____

_____

_____

"Father, hallowed be your name, your kingdom come. Give us each day our daily bread. Forgive us our sins, for we also forgive everyone who sins against us. And lead us not into temptation."

LUKE 11:2–4 NIV

New prayer requests:

Date:

Ongoing prayer requests:

Answers to prayer: _____

_____

_____

_____

_____

_____

_____

_____

_____

_____

Praises: _____

_____

_____

_____

_____

_____

_____

_____

_____

_____

_____

_____

I love them that love me;
and those that seek me early shall find me.

PROVERBS 8:17

New prayer requests: _____

Date: _____

Ongoing prayer requests: _____

Answers to prayer: _____

_____

_____

_____

_____

_____

_____

_____

_____

_____

_____

_____

Praises: _____

_____

_____

_____

_____

_____

_____

_____

_____

_____

_____

_____

If I regard iniquity in my heart,
the Lord will not hear me.

PSALM 66:18

New prayer requests:

Date:

Ongoing prayer requests:

Answers to prayer: ─────────────────────────────────

──
──
──
──
──
──
──
──
──
──

Praises: ──

──
──
──
──
──
──
──
──
──
──

And at midnight Paul and Silas prayed, and sang praises unto God: and the prisoners heard them.

ACTS 16:25

New prayer requests: _____

_____

_____

_____

_____

_____

_____

_____

_____

_____

_____

Date: _____

Ongoing prayer requests: _____

_____

_____

_____

_____

_____

_____

_____

_____

_____

_____

Answers to prayer: _____

_____

_____

_____

_____

_____

_____

_____

_____

Praises: _____

_____

_____

_____

_____

_____

_____

_____

_____

_____

_____

Pray for the peace of Jerusalem:

they shall prosper that love thee.

PSALM 122:6

New prayer requests: _____

_____

_____

_____

_____

_____

_____

_____

_____

_____

_____

_____

Date: _____

Ongoing prayer requests: _____

_____

_____

_____

_____

_____

_____

_____

_____

_____

_____

_____

Answers to prayer:

Praises:

"But I tell you: Love your enemies and pray for those who persecute you, that you may be sons of your Father in heaven."

MATTHEW 5:44–45 NIV

New prayer requests: _____

_____

_____

_____

_____

_____

_____

_____

_____

_____

_____

_____

Date: _____

Ongoing prayer requests: _____

_____

_____

_____

_____

_____

_____

_____

_____

_____

_____

_____

Answers to prayer: _____

_____

_____

_____

_____

_____

_____

_____

_____

_____

_____

Praises: _____

_____

_____

_____

_____

_____

_____

_____

_____

_____

_____

_____

Rejoice evermore.
Pray without ceasing.

1 THESSALONIANS 5:16–17

New prayer requests: _____

Date: _____

Ongoing prayer requests: _____

Answers to prayer:

_____
_____
_____
_____
_____
_____
_____
_____
_____
_____

Praises:

_____
_____
_____
_____
_____
_____
_____
_____
_____
_____
_____

We have not stopped praying for you and asking God to fill you with the knowledge of his will through all spiritual wisdom and understanding.

COLOSSIANS 1:9 NIV

Date:

New prayer requests:

Ongoing prayer requests:

Answers to prayer: _____

Praises: _____

"But as for me and my household,
we will serve the Lord."

JOSHUA 24:15 NIV

New prayer requests: _____

Date:

Ongoing prayer requests: _____

Answers to prayer: _____

_____

_____

_____

_____

_____

_____

_____

_____

_____

_____

Praises: _____

_____

_____

_____

_____

_____

_____

_____

_____

_____

_____

She named him Samuel, saying,
"Because I asked the LORD for him."

1 SAMUEL 1:20 NIV

New prayer requests:

Date:

Ongoing prayer requests:

Answers to prayer: _____

_____
_____
_____
_____
_____
_____
_____
_____
_____
_____
_____
_____

Praises: _____

_____
_____
_____
_____
_____
_____
_____
_____
_____
_____
_____
_____
_____

"Which of you, if his son asks for bread, will give him a stone?
Or if he asks for a fish, will give him a snake?"

MATTHEW 7:9–10 NIV

Date: _____

New prayer requests: _____

_____

_____

_____

_____

_____

_____

_____

_____

_____

_____

Ongoing prayer requests: _____

_____

_____

_____

_____

_____

_____

_____

_____

_____

_____

_____

Answers to prayer: _____

Praises: _____

"Be always on the watch, and pray that you may be able to escape all that is about to happen, and that you may be able to stand before the Son of Man."

LUKE 21:36 NIV

Date: _____

New prayer requests: _____

Ongoing prayer requests: _____

Answers to prayer: _____

_____

_____

_____

_____

_____

_____

_____

_____

_____

_____

_____

Praises: _____

_____

_____

_____

_____

_____

_____

_____

_____

_____

_____

_____

"I tell you that in the same way there will be more rejoicing in heaven over one sinner who repents than over ninety-nine righteous persons who do not need to repent."

LUKE 15:7 NIV

New prayer requests: _____

Date: _____

Ongoing prayer requests: _____

Answers to prayer: _____

_____

_____

_____

_____

_____

_____

_____

_____

_____

_____

Praises: _____

_____

_____

_____

_____

_____

_____

_____

_____

_____

_____

_____

Remain in me,
and I will remain in you.

JOHN 15:4 NIV

New prayer requests: _____

Ongoing prayer requests: _____

Date: _____

Answers to prayer: _____

_____

_____

_____

_____

_____

_____

_____

_____

_____

_____

_____

Praises: _____

_____

_____

_____

_____

_____

_____

_____

_____

_____

_____

_____

"Because you have seen me, you have believed;
blessed are those who have not seen and yet have believed."

JOHN 20:29 NIV

New prayer requests: _____

Date: _____

Ongoing prayer requests: _____

Answers to prayer: _____

_____

_____

_____

_____

_____

_____

_____

_____

_____

_____

Praises: _____

_____

_____

_____

_____

_____

_____

_____

_____

_____

_____

_____

New prayer requests:

Date:

Ongoing prayer requests:

Answers to prayer: _____

_____

_____

_____

_____

_____

_____

_____

_____

_____

_____

_____

Praises: _____

_____

_____

_____

_____

_____

_____

_____

_____

_____

_____

_____

Blessed is he whose transgressions are forgiven, whose sins are covered.
Blessed is the man whose sin the LORD does not count against him.

PSALM 32:1–2 NIV

Date:

New prayer requests:

Ongoing prayer requests:

Answers to prayer: _____
_____
_____
_____
_____
_____
_____
_____
_____
_____
_____
_____
_____

Praises: _____
_____
_____
_____
_____
_____
_____
_____
_____
_____
_____
_____
_____
_____

That if you confess with your mouth, "Jesus is Lord,"
and believe in your heart that God raised him from the dead, you will be saved.

ROMANS 10:9 NIV

New prayer requests:

_____

_____

_____

_____

_____

_____

_____

_____

_____

_____

Date: _____

Ongoing prayer requests:

_____

_____

_____

_____

_____

_____

_____

_____

_____

_____

Answers to prayer:

Praises:

But because Jesus lives forever, he has a permanent priesthood.
Therefore he is able to save completely those who come to God through him,
because he always lives to intercede for them.

HEBREWS 7:24–25 NIV

New prayer requests: _____

_____
_____
_____
_____
_____
_____
_____
_____
_____
_____
_____
_____

Ongoing prayer requests: _____

_____
_____
_____
_____
_____
_____
_____
_____
_____
_____
_____
_____
_____

Date: _____

Answers to prayer: _____

_____

_____

_____

_____

_____

_____

_____

_____

_____

_____

Praises: _____

_____

_____

_____

_____

_____

_____

_____

_____

_____

_____

Therefore we do not lose heart. Though outwardly we are wasting away,
yet inwardly we are being renewed day by day.

2 CORINTHIANS 4:16 NIV

New prayer requests: _____

Date: _____

Ongoing prayer requests: _____

Answers to prayer:

Praises:

And I pray that you. . .may have power, with all the saints,
to grasp how wide and long and high and deep is the love of Christ.

EPHESIANS 3:17–18 NIV

New prayer requests:

Ongoing prayer requests:

Date:

Answers to prayer: _____

_____

_____

_____

_____

_____

_____

_____

_____

_____

_____

_____

Praises: _____

_____

_____

_____

_____

_____

_____

_____

_____

_____

_____

_____

_____

And pray in the Spirit on all occasions with all kinds of prayers and requests.
With this in mind, be alert and always keep on praying for all the saints.

New prayer requests: _____

Date:

_____
_____
_____
_____
_____
_____
_____
_____
_____
_____
_____
_____

Ongoing prayer requests: _____

_____
_____
_____
_____
_____
_____
_____
_____
_____
_____
_____
_____
_____

Answers to prayer: _____

_____
_____
_____
_____
_____
_____
_____
_____
_____
_____
_____

Praises: _____

_____
_____
_____
_____
_____
_____
_____
_____
_____
_____
_____
_____

But ye are a chosen generation, a royal priesthood, an holy nation,
a peculiar people: that ye should shew forth the praises of him
who hath called you out of darkness into his marvellous light.

1 PETER 2:9

Date:

New prayer requests:

Ongoing prayer requests:

Answers to prayer: _____

_____

_____

_____

_____

_____

_____

_____

_____

_____

_____

Praises: _____

_____

_____

_____

_____

_____

_____

_____

_____

_____

_____

_____

And when ye stand praying, forgive, if ye have ought against any: that your Father also which is in heaven may forgive you your trespasses.

MARK 11:25

New prayer requests: _____

Date: _____

Ongoing prayer requests: _____

Answers to prayer: _____

_____
_____
_____
_____
_____
_____
_____
_____
_____
_____
_____

Praises: _____

_____
_____
_____
_____
_____
_____
_____
_____
_____
_____
_____
_____

So then, just as you received Christ Jesus as Lord,

continue to live in him, rooted and built up in him,

strengthened in the faith as you were taught, and overflowing with thankfulness.

COLOSSIANS 2:6 NIV

New prayer requests: _____

_____

_____

_____

_____

_____

_____

_____

_____

_____

_____

Date: _____

Ongoing prayer requests: _____

_____

_____

_____

_____

_____

_____

_____

_____

_____

_____

_____

_____

Answers to prayer: _____

Praises: _____

Set your minds on things above,

not on earthly things.

COLOSSIANS 3:2 NIV

New prayer requests: _____

Date: _____

Ongoing prayer requests: _____

Answers to prayer: _____

_____
_____
_____
_____
_____
_____
_____
_____
_____
_____

Praises: _____

_____
_____
_____
_____
_____
_____
_____
_____
_____
_____
_____

Now to him who is able to do immeasurably more than all we ask or imagine, according to his power that is at work within us, to him be glory in the church and in Christ Jesus throughout all generations, for ever and ever! Amen.

EPHESIANS 3:20–21 NIV

Date:

New prayer requests: _____

_____

_____

_____

_____

_____

_____

_____

_____

_____

_____

Ongoing prayer requests: _____

_____

_____

_____

_____

_____

_____

_____

_____

_____

_____